Heading Toward Silver Dust

Poems on Aging

Martha Deborah Hall

Plain View Press
http://plainviewpress.net

3800 N. Lamar, Suite 730-260
Austin, TX 78756

Copyright © 2012 Martha Deborah Hall. All rights reserved under International and Pan-American Copyright Conventions. No part of this book may be reproduced or distributed in any form or by any means, or stored in a data base or retrieval system, without written permission from the author. All rights, including electronic, are reserved by the author and publisher.

ISBN: 978-1-935514-56-5
Library of Congress Control Number: 2012950155

Cover Art: Kathleen Andrews Memorial Bench
          Photograph by Martha Deborah Hall
Cover Design: Pam Knight

Acknowledgments

Some of the poems in this collection previously appeared in: Silver Dust, published by Indigo Mosaic.

In loving memory of

Kathleen Duval Andrews

Augusta Bloom

Betty Hall

Phyllis Yudickey

who taught us how to live and die

with poignant grace

Contents

Part One: My Prayer — 7

Shoreline	9
On Life's Raft	10
980 Whalley Avenue	11
Walking Through After	12
In the Cherry Bureau with the Cold Marble Top	13
My Audubon List	14
Old Age Sonata	15
Pipe Dreams	16
No Via Rupta	17
Poolside	18
Yesterday Had a Twin Sister	19
My Ragdoll	20
Checkmate	21
From Colt to Mane-Tangled Mare	22
Downswing	23
In the Glass	24
No Hook	25
Ten Things I Loved About You, Twenty Years Ago	26
From a Parachute	27
To Freeze or Not	28
Viagra, Anyone?	29
No Joy Stick	30
Root Canal	31
Spring Cleaning	32
History of My Heart	33
Dans Ma Cuisine	34
My Prayer	35

Part Two: What We Learned — 37

My Altar	39
Dear Death	41
May's Fourth Monday	42
Weeds	43
In Your Living Room	45
Grandmothers' Quotes	46
Do or Dew	48
Way Out?	49
P.O.W. at 88	50

Dying Is Part of Living	51
Countdown	52
Sunday Morning	53
Minnie Bourke-White	54
Bits	55
Waiting at 70	56
On the Couch at 70	57
Brownout	58
Grains	59
With Bone Cancer	60
Octogenarian in Hospice	61
What We Learned	62
Class Acts	63
So Long	64
Aged Cardboard Masks	65
Final Inning	66

Part Three: Before the Last Shoe Drops 67

Apart at the Seams	69
Taps?	70
Before I Lay Me Down to Sleep	71
Christmas Gifts in Year-Round Wraps	72
Remember Me?	74
Let Your Hands Be	75
In Order	76
My Retirement Vacation	77
Red-Roofed Retirement Cave	78
Before the Last Shoe Drops	79
Clone This	80
Not Old Fogeys	81
January Mantra	82
Like Cheetahs	83
Coffin Pillow Talk	84
Whose Engine Will My Leftover Car Keys Start?	85
"Keys That Are Used Do Not Rust"	86

About the Author　　　　　　　　　　　　　　　87

Part One:
My Prayer

Shoreline

Alone near the edge
of the ocean, as a CD
of 1963 Billboard Top Pop Hits
plays, for the hundredth time,
"I'm Leaving It Up to You."
Acts I and II, the beginning and middle
of my life, blend into the third act,
old age—my final aria.

Resonances of internal operas,
of past pain and happiness, chant.
Melodies of broken heart-strands
resurge and then fade. Vibrant
sonatas of what was my being
end in discord and then resurrect.
Sonorous Methodist church-organ hymns
of my youth play along in my mind.

An anchor of emptiness, secured
in the sanctuary of the ocean floor,
breaks loose and what's left of its life
washes toward me. A chipped seashell,
left in the sand, with holes broken through
its shiny surface, beckons and greets me.
Its spiral rings, swirling upward
in an arrow-like point, guide my spirit
in that direction.

Martha Deborah Hall
On Life's Raft

After low, high tide will follow.
One must hold onto love's anchor.
Swim away from all things shallow.
After low, high tide will follow.
Do not surface like dead flounder.
Swim gallantly into life's shores.
After low, high tide will follow.
Never let go of love's anchor.

980 Whalley Avenue

Then:
    Aida arias chanted.
    Hot chocolate, brewed
    in the Corningware pot,
    was always topped with tons
    of whipped cream. Family
    photos greeted me when I woke up;
    the furnace puffed; sun-soaked
    brick walls reflected heat, warmed
    the inside; granite headers
    reverberated colonial charm.
    A three-car garage held my Jaguar.
    It was charming to read by the fire
    at day's end. In the family room
    after school let out, the kids and I
    watched Carol Burnett.
    A well-established architect
    and his family lived next door.

Now:
    Absorbed into twelve-over-twelve
    window frames, sonata notes
    cascade down the hall, try to enter
    under closed bedroom doors, but don't.
    They ultimately fall flat on cold
    basement floors. The fireplace needs
    a new liner. In the family room
    I see a mouse cornered by my cat.
    Ring stains from my daily supper cups
    of soup mar the cherry end table.
    My new neighbor has been dubbed
    "a stalker."

Martha Deborah Hall
Walking Through After

    Outside your classic Victorian with cupola,
a vintage green and lemon spade…a snow-
flake and then, drops of rain. Inside, your brush
next to never-sold paintings…eyeglasses in
silver frames…a tiger-eyed marble on a Lenox
dish…a plastic spoon in the hot chocolate tin, left-
over thread from the drapes you sewed…I'm still
grappling.

In the Cherry Bureau with the Cold Marble Top

At nine years old, after my mother died,
I opened the top drawer and hugged to my chest
a white, silk slip which bore no scent. I reminisced:
Shalimar.

Decades later, in its middle drawer,
I spied a small silver case. My old engagement ring
sneered: "Why did you have to place me here?
Look in your mirror, reply."

One day the bottom drawer jammed on the left side.
I couldn't budge it open, my old fingers split
and chapped. I'll try again in the spring.

Martha Deborah Hall
My Audubon List

I don't want to go as a whooping crane, long-
eared nosey owl, pygmy or peer caw parrot,
or yellow-breasted chat. No thrasher catbird, hermit
thrush, no mockingbird, nut-hatch, water pipit,
or ruffled grouse. Keep from my pear tree
the little hermit, black-capped tyrant, gray-crowned
yellow throat, and common screech wild turkey.
Let me cede with the grace of a swan. You be my
mourning dove.

Old Age Sonata

> *It's not how many times you get knocked down but how many times you get up.*
> — Cybill Shepherd

View twelve-inch snowstorms as dustings.
Put on your boots, slosh through life's gales.
In yourself you must be trusting.
View twelve-inch snowstorms as dustings.
Righteous paths, no adjusting.
Your principles do not impale.
View twelve-inch snowstorms as dustings.
Put on your boots, stomp through those gales.

Martha Deborah Hall
Pipe Dreams

As a child I heard: In the future, tomorrow, some day,
down the road, the when you do this and then that,
the bye n' byes, the promises from above,
all will burn in your life, filter into your being.
You won't end in a "Marlboro Country" grave,
be a Camel alone in the desert, but mentholated
with a fragrant column of smoke at your finish,
wafting through you. Just be good, be polite
like a Philip Morris bellhop, Pall Mall, do onto others,
life will sing. Addictions to good things won't yellow
your teeth if you proceed along an exhaust-free path;
you'll not relapse nor need Nicoderm. Sparkle up
with a Zippo lighter, blow smoke rings that glide
to the top, rise above life's stacks of soot. Your match
not extinguished, your luminescence will glow.
As you age, like the last puff of a Virginia Slim,
you'll leave a menthol-like trail, flick life's bad
carbon away, stash it in a ceramic-topped ash tray.
Don't think of the then and the when. Close the door
to harmful toxins; proceed to act in your now. Be
a marijuana shoot grown in the soil, nourish, give pleasure
to others, waft high in each separate fragrance
you've worked for. Become a beautiful, treasured weed.

No Via Rupta

How many miles must we tread
to reach Summit Peak? At the end
will our souls have been polished
as with Old English
to bring out our natural inner beauty?

Looking back down our road,
have we done our best
to plant Van Gogh sunflowers?
Have we journeyed with pride
over life's trail as if dressed
for an eternal marriage
to what's ethical and fair?

Have we jumped with zest
Off the diving boards of ponds,
proud of well-worn swimsuits?
As we achieve our sunset
and head toward silver dust
what will be our testimony?

Martha Deborah Hall
Poolside

Reality sets in at two-thirty this morning
during a session of REM. The scene takes place
around an outdoor swimming pool
that looks freshly chlorinated, pristine

and sky-blue. Old friends laze around the edges;
my twin sister sunbathes on the diving board.
Containers of popcorn and pretzels
rest on side tables along with plastic glasses

filled with vanilla milk shakes. There are bodies
on the bottom of the pool. Arms gently waft
like minnows. Lips seem to move and suck in
cold water as trout do. No words spoken,

no splashes, squeals of youth, rubbing of inner tubes
against side walls. No nosey neighbors peeping
from windows. My REM lens zeroes in;
faces become clear. Bathing suit colors,

appropriate to personalities, engulf my vision.
I stare and then reality swims inward,
showing faces of friends and family
who are dead.

Yesterday Had a Twin Sister

I wish you were back. There are so few
people I take time-outs with. You were
my needle without cocaine, the spark
I should have mimicked in so many ways,
the embellishment of life's good, wrapped
in the ideal of Christmas giving. You pranced
as a reindeer with a gliding light, accepted life's
transgressions as if they had only the strength
of a melting snowball thrown by a child. With
you here, there would be no frost on my window
panes. You'd help me keep venturing-out skaters
on dangerous ponds in our lives safe from harm.

Martha Deborah Hall
My Ragdoll

Feathers
float on their way
down to earth. Once again
I am an entity of one,
not two.

Checkmate

Gone are the days
when I could fall asleep
holding onto a New York City
subway strap on the way home
from work, or the nights
when I'd slink into slumber
at 8 o'clock, fatigued from being
creative (in thought at least)
while dabbing with Ajax,
Fab, and Palmolive, scintillating
tools of motherhood.
Gone the late nights
of Johnny Carson, Jack Paar,
Sinatra, and Lauren Bacall.

At seventy I nod off in my cocoa-
colored bedroom. At first, the sleep
angel triumphs. Three or four hours
later, the wake-up demon arrives.
Bedroom days of you-King, me-Queen
have flown. I've turned into something
like a celibate bishop or a pawn
in this game, cheated
out of one of life's prized possessions.
Neither whole grain rice, bananas, warm milk,
nor a turkey BLT help. Many nights I open
a vial of Sonata, roll a pill
down my throat and win the game.

Martha Deborah Hall
From Colt to Mane-Tangled Mare

Prancing
through each decade,
trotting across blonde fields,
whinnying as old oat buckets
run out.

Downswing

With false teeth I'm in the rumble seat
on the way to my life's dance. Years ago
he'd be in light blues, I in knockout pinks.
Today you'll see us dressed in dowdy,
dank-dark browns. If he wants soup,
I say, "Campbell's." If I want sex,
he's out of Viagra. Nothing
is wonderful. We paid the fiddler
for our climb to the top. Our lives
remind me of garbage-in/garbage-out.
Our waltz ended years ago. He took me
off his American Girl list. I shoo him
to the gym each day. He closes—no—slams
the door on his way to the garage.
I pop a melatonin.

Martha Deborah Hall
In the Glass

Worn-out
toothbrush in hand,
hair curlers dangling down,
I stare in mirror: wrinkles, no
dentures.

No Hook

Look through
life's rear mirror.
What have *you* seen out there?
Something *I* refuse to let in —
old age.

Martha Deborah Hall

Ten Things I Loved About You, Twenty Years Ago

1. You made me coffee in bed every morning,
2. You were gentle but strong.
3. You never stopped until daily chores were finished.
4. You did all the driving on winter trips to Florida.
5. You devoured my pre-cooked hams.
6. You were skipper of our sailboat, racing around the Isles of Shoals.
7. You placed flowers on my mother's grave on the anniversary of her death.
8. You took over the two A.M. feedings of each one of our three children.
9. You joined me in chocolate splurges on Sunday afternoons.
10. You shut the door quietly on the way out.

From a Parachute

He was a keeper,
a Christmas bow I wanted
wrapped around my finger,
my aphrodisiac cologne
on springtime evenings in bed,
a blue wash cloth that wiped away
my tears, my beach umbrella
on August dog days. One frosty night
his mother-in-law, with broom
and silver hair, dropped in.
My marriage became entangled
and then ended.

Martha Deborah Hall
To Freeze or Not

After leaving the Nashua Country Club
on Wednesday afternoons during 1988,
he'd end up in the lobby of the Crowne
Plaza Hotel. Quite often he'd sit next to me
or my friend in a black leather chair. He sported
a smile of gorgeous whites, kept a private plane
at the Nashua Airport and would often fly
South during New Hampshire winters. I wanted
a relationship but was awestruck and intimidated.
In January of 2011, I heard on a national newscast
that this famous baseball player, Ted Williams,
had written in his will his desire to be cremated.
Several of his children are fighting over
whether they should continue to keep him
in biostasis (frozen) so they can all be together
after they pass. Yikes. Glad he didn't hit on me.

Viagra, Anyone?

So long
to my sex drive,
former havoc wreaker.
Hello to life's new appearance,
ennui.

Martha Deborah Hall
No Joy Stick

What's the sense of loving? They only go away.

Gone the zigs, the zags, the spurts in life.
Yesterday's shoes stand empty in my closet.
The only photo left on my dresser is of us.
I've stashed our memories under the mattress,
closed roads to bridges we ran across.
Wasted away are the good foods in life,
especially you, my whipped cream.
Now dismissive and bitter, the once wild me
feels kicked under the bus since you died.
Decembers are hard without you by the fire,
sparkles gone from my Fourth of July.
I feel dead from the neck up.
Will words to each other sway in the wind
once we've rotted, our love story,
our most precious possession,
be stashed in the barn bay?

Root Canal

You bond in anger more than love.
Break down its walls, then you will sing.
Be free of fuss and sing, my dove.
You bond in anger more than love.
Seal in concrete all metal gloves.
Bequeath yourself a signet ring.
Why bond in anger more than love?
Break down its walls and you will sing.

Martha Deborah Hall
Spring Cleaning

> ...*happiness is in quiet things, not in the peaks of ecstasy.*
> —Anais Nin

So recall the bird song,
the splash of cold water
running from July's faucet,
the lime-colored glass
filled with lemonade.
Place Häagen-Dazs
in a Sunday bowl
and waltz it to your mouth
on a silver spoon. Go to bed
at nine on Monday. On Tuesday
make crème brûlée for others.
Have buttered popcorn at Susan's
on Wednesday. Put time aside
on Thursday for a walk
with chatty friends. On Friday
see an old-time movie
at the Wilton Town Hall.
Let yourself have three slices
of pepperoni pizza on Saturday.
Empty transgression-filled barrels,
suck your voice out from the rug.
Sew together and then iron
ripped seams of your heart.
Shovel away unfounded fears,
mow green grass for your prom.
Wet mop floors, use soapy water
to drown life's weeds. Dust up
your feathers, bleach sins white,
wash all guilt away. Polish your good,
throw old hurts in the hamper. It's time
to go out and play.

History of My Heart

Musical chords slammed against walls.
Arteries clogged by mud.
Valves drained into empty streets.
Clotted blood cadence.
Thump beneath my wings.

Martha Deborah Hall
Dans Ma Cuisine

> *Maybe we're happy ten minutes in the day.*
> — Edith Piaf in the film, *A Passionate Life*

Feed me bonbons, pâte de foie gras, pommes de grace, and ratatouille.
Let me focus on quiche lorraine, crème brûlée, petits fours.
Slide me fromage, pain au gratin, chocolat, brioche.
Wake me with croissants, amandé tartes, le pain, and pinot noir.
Involve me with pommes de terre, coq au vin.
Ease me, fill my void.

My Prayer

Allow me to be comfortable in the room called me.
Give me courage to dance alone in the parlor when I want to.
Let me run free like a mare in an open field. Let me be
the woman who remembers that at one end of life
there's a Davis Lane, at the other a cemetery. Let me toss
life's rotted boards in the trash, then construct new foundations.
Allow my essence to screech like smoke from a chimney
on a blustery day, to reject the auto-pilot easy way. Let me submerge
the sniffle factor in the bath, be comfortable in the self I call
home.

Part Two:
What We Learned

My Altar

Ten dog years into it, alone
in my condo, rain plinks
on my black asphalt roof.

With cell phone, the internet,
but no teddy bears on my dashboard,
I'm on Facebook, and happy within

the museum called me. In the last
several weeks, when free, I've spent
hours polishing cherished items

that would tell a visitor about who I am.
There's a five-foot brass coat rack
at the entrance, from which dangle

favorite coats from L. L. Bean,
along with down ski mittens, a favorite
Ralph Lauren silk scarf.

There's an old brass boot holder
from an 18th century shoemaker,
a large copper bucket

into which I kick off my shoes
when I walk in the door. Glowing gently
are candlesticks holding maroon soys,

a Gucci clock, a fireplace
with an old brick hearth, and a cherished
mortar and pestle rarely used anymore

for grinding garlic. In my bedroom are two
vintage cherry bureaus, one from his family,
one from mine, covered with marble tops.

In my living room, on an antique table,
rests a pewter ice cream mold in the shape
of a flower. The other half of the set, a pear,

is kept on the mantle in my niece's home.
She lives one block away. My unit is filled
with antiques waiting to be taken by children

as soon as they have enough room. My 32-inch
Panasonic TV is usually turned off.
Hymns from my youth often cascade

through the rooms. In my granite-countered
kitchen, I have one plate, one peach-colored
coffee cup, one fork, one self.

Dear Death

My insides are dressed in black. I can't stay the course, climb mountain peaks, or believe time will heal. I can't wash doomsday away, or stop bawling at night. I can't "do it to it," can't remove my grey veil and gloves. I can't be me, unwind you, be on the high side of bi-polar. I can't expose my soul, my self. I feel like a dried-out stuffed turkey, turds in a cesspool, a Christmas tree at the dump. I can't get out of bed, humor life with good old boy's brouhaha. Dear Death, give me more time to mourn. Dear Death, go drop dead.

Martha Deborah Hall
May's Fourth Monday

Dead roses in a pewter vase on the counter.
A paint can for use in the family room is dented
on its left side. Music starts up outside
though I heard the baton twirler has a cold
and the former razzmatazz bugler recently left town.
Old vets, I see, are still marching. As my heart tries to
beat to clanging cymbals, I ask where's the roll
of my drum, the me in the bandstands of former marches,
the star-spangled banner blares of my parades.
Notes inside my corps seem sopped and muffled
by wet confetti. I move steadily in step with the others,
advance out to my garden to weed. Precious petals
smashed in last night's rain ceremony need yanking.
Poison ivy salutes near a border of grass.
A box of unused fire crackers need to explode into action.
My Memorial Day ceremony clogs on by.

Weeds

If looking back at my life for the last time,
I wouldn't think of receiving my giddy college diplomas
or storming highways in Great Gatsby-type cars.

I wouldn't think of being on Jerry Lewis' telethon
and then exiting to the crowd outside the studio
who waited for our autographs. (They didn't see us

as we slipped down the side street to ride home
on the subway.) In my binocular vision of importance,
it wouldn't be the night when I was Ronald Reagan's

Campaign Chairman for my town, and he won
the presidency, or when I worked as Alexander Haig's
Communications Director. I don't regret my attitude

toward schmucks or toward the back-and-forth
ping pong jerks laid out on my voyage table.
I'll brush aside the microwave types that took a minute

to cook, then cool. But what I will carry
from the last breaths of life to my crematorium
are guilty feelings for transgressions toward others.

They're the soured lollipops of my existence,
not roses but my weeds. Once, I screeched at my twin
when she refused to stop smoking, even though

it was too late by then to make any difference.
I wasn't gracious when she took a train to Ohio
to see me. I left her to entertain herself, while I played

important student. Doug Wauchope came from New York
to Ohio to visit me on one of his West Point vacations,
and, as soon as he arrived, I suggested he go home

because I was interested in someone else.
He was later blown up in Vietnam by a grenade
whose pin caught on his Jeep's handle. I'm ashamed

of the time I stole a twenty-dollar bill
from my mother's purse, as well as when I pulled dishes
off the dining room table to the floor. I'll remember

giving verbal acceptance to a friend,
who threw seven golden retriever puppies into a river
to drown. It's the dark weather I've caused

in the lives of others that makes my heart pound
with shame. Did these transgressions help me learn
to become a better person? You'll have to decide.

In Your Living Room

Can you swerve from the left to the right
in bad weather? Can you plough your way
through the rough? Can you give mutual respect
when not due? Can you stop with the silliness of April
fools? Can you face where you're going for once?
Can you survive tropical depressions? Can you last
for an instant beyond hurt? Can you remember
one good-bye could be the last? Can you stop tiring
of your dreams? Can you empty clean your behavior?
Can you, can you, can you, when in the house
of your dying they say you did or you didn't?

Martha Deborah Hall
Grandmothers' Quotes

For my grandchildren from LaLa

What the Grandmothers Said:
    Rainy days are good for making cookies.
    Something good comes from everything that happens.
    This too shall pass.
    Some day they'll have a cure for schizophrenia.
    Grandmothers take over the rocking chairs and sit looking out sliding glass doors after grandfathers
    are gone.
    The worm will turn.
    It must be nice.

What I Say:
    Always check the zippers on sale items.
    Interview the interviewer.
    Don't hold keys over drains.
    You can't return to yesterday.
    An operatic aria is a reminder that the world is not about me.
    Wash the milk bottle off before putting it in the fridge.
    People who hide their name badges usually don't give good service.
    Snow slides quicker off a steep roof.
    Foundation snow keeps cold air out.
    Save electricity: unplug your computers.
    Stand up straight for what you believe in.
    If moving to another house, take your EcoFlow showerhead with you.
    The person who lives the furthest away is often the first to arrive.
    Look in and out of windows, then look inside and stay.
    Load dryer racks from bottom to top.
    Use the showerhead as a water pic.
    Buy your Band-Aids at the Dollar Store.
    If you put tools away, you'll know where to find them.
    Things don't buy happiness but they help.

Note: Phrases in the poem "Grandmothers' Quotes" are credited to the following people:

Elizabeth Whilmas: *Rainy days are good for making cookies.*

Marion Schofield: *Something good comes from everything that happens.*

Elizabeth Whitman: *This too shall pass.*

Hex Hall: *Grandmothers take over the rocking chairs and sit looking out sliding glass doors after grandfathers are gone.*

Beverley Mancini: *The worm will turn.*

Alice Gilman: *It must be nice.*

Martha Deborah Hall
Do or Dew

When the band plays, I march to the top. It costs.
I was the team, the ruby star, the new-mown blade.
I was the person with white-ironed socks,
then the one who owned a patio with heated bird bath,
the one with a Mercedes, Jaguar and Jeep.
Now, at eighty-four, I'm not sure who-for-what I'm meant.
Perhaps writing can become my Seine River.
Bingo doesn't do it. Decades old skis languish at the lean-to.
Antiques gather mold in the barn. Playing Chopin doesn't inspire.
A friend's Christmas e-card takes too long to load. Darn! Silver
needs polishing again. The spirit of the season mocks-stomps me.
I know to get anything done, I'll need to get out of bed
but don't want to. With no day-before transgressions to blame,
I wake every morning exhausted. Life is garbage-in/garbage-out.
I start to plan my next year's budget ($2,000 for my teeth,
an extra $100 for my especially dry hair) but I notice a ceiling stain.
Then I go to lunch with a friend, talk to her of the heart attack symptoms
I'm having at the table. I recover, then ask, "Where are we going
shopping today?"

Way Out?

I want to ditch my Subaru,
get rid of dust-collector antiques,
logs never burned in fires, Lenox china
in glass-faced cupboards, clothes that screech,
"I want out," grocery bags from Wal-Mart
filling a bin, never read books, unused hair bands
purchased for holidays, tools I don't know how
to operate, blankets for unused doubles,
skis that bore me to smithereens.
Go homeless? Nah…

Martha Deborah Hall
P.O.W. at 88

Neighbor
passes by me
on my way to office.
I ask, "How's your life?" She replies,
"I'm bored."

Dying Is Part of Living

Drool spills on matted beard. Old slacks languish in the closet.
Eyebrows stick straight up. Age spots glare in the morning sun.
Eyeglasses on the end table are smeared with egg. Gnarled hands
have broken fingernails. Gray hair lies askew on the pillow.
A medicine-filled catheter stands next to his bed and near his black
wheelchair. The wooden cane, once used at Pearl Street, is off
in a corner. On a white-painted shelf are unopened books
laden with cobwebs. Chopin cascades through the hallway.
I sit next to this dyer, support him on his trip into the unknown.

Martha Deborah Hall
Countdown

If I
had one hour of
time left, one thing I am
certain of: I would not spend it
with you.

Sunday Morning

Hourglass sand drips seconds.

Martha Deborah Hall
Minnie Bourke-White

Like Ted Kooser's "Early Bird,"
mother is downstairs on a cold May morning.
I lie in bed, mulling over some of the lessons
she gave me in childhood: Be fearless, believe
in problem solving, work toward your dreams,
know what you want from your art.
She used to say: doors close but others do open,
be sure to thank God (just in case), try to spend
quiet times by splashing in fountains, be a lighted
lantern, not just another pea in the pod,
be everywhere you're needed, wear many hats
(and shoes), random acts of kindness are marvelous,
wasted time is that, don't depend on him
to make you happy, the past is passed, wake up
with thoughts of the future in your head, be your own
rules and boundaries, go play, burn your hates in ovens,
survive your losses, go to the sea and dive into its waves,
swim in the nude for yourself, hunger for alternatives,
refuse to accept unhappiness, buy multi-colored umbrellas
for the rains, dream your dream, act in your act,
don't be a leaf peeper but seed your own crimson maples,
soar on the wings of each morning and remember it *isn't* over
until the fat lady sings. Guess I'd better get up.

Bits

Inside the physician's atrium,
a Christmas tree tilts. Grey bows
droop, wrinkled and stained.
An angel near a bottom branch
misses a white sleeve. The sterling
silver box on the receptionist's desk
needs polishing. The piped-in Christmas
carol ends. Four older people wait
in the lobby next to the door with a sign:
"Psychiatrist."

Martha Deborah Hall
Waiting at 70

Thursday
they'll do one more
non-invasive(?) ultra-
sound of the lump Dr. Chan found.
Cancer?

On the Couch at 70

"Have compassion for each emotion you feel.
Try to accept the few you hate. I said try. Did you

hear me? Release feelings that no longer serve.

I know you despise that pain at work, the self-
imposed micro/mini manager. Forget her. Rise above.

Are you listening? Stay in the present. Let kindness
enter. Be spontaneous. Accept change. Be yourself.

Now let's go back to the anger you have

against the dude in your poetry class. Surrender
to what is. Embrace each moment as a miracle,

and give thanks for what's important."

The beep of her watch tells me my hour's up.
On my way home, I still want to strangle the jerks.

Martha Deborah Hall
Brownout

If I start
to cry,
I'm afraid
I'll never stop.

Grains

Ice edges out toward offshore rocks. I glare
through windows, recall days of what

were supposed to be smooth sailing,
then attempt to shore up my spirit.

Sadness spills from my heart, tears down
my sandcastles. I try to wash away

the past, hold on to the lapping present,
gain a foothold, but I flounder

and flap on life's ocean floor. Abandoned
in the face of truth, I believe if I choose to

drown myself, my body, my soul, my life,
will finally gain buoyancy.

Martha Deborah Hall
With Bone Cancer

I climb
stairs to my room.
In bed my heart's throbbing.
I am going to die *and do
not care.*

Octogenarian in Hospice

Act deaf.
But Listen.
Can you
Finally
Hear Life
Kicking
Me in
My soul?

Martha Deborah Hall
What We Learned

Across the brook's swinging bridge,
up to the top of the hill and then munching
our lunch, we saw a soothing group of cows
in a golden summer field. They were our stars,
our own quiet beacons. One moo suggested
we were welcomed. Some strayed apart
from others in their search for life's sweetest
grass. They taught us a good overall plan:
to avoid life's dung, learn to walk around,
not in it. Throughout the decades we still
spied them. We tried to proceed undeterred
in our fields, to not be part of the herd,
to swirl our cowlicks, like them, into a smooth
pattern, to be our own purple cows.

Class Acts

1.

A ninety-ish woman
with white hair
drives her purple
PT Cruiser quickly
around the Milford
Oval. Her handicap
license plate reads,
"I CAN."

2.

Shooting toward me
on 101 East, running
faster than I have seen,
an old man jogs
in my direction. His dog
looks worn to a frazzle.
They stop and the master
feeds his dog a biscuit.
They continue
running.

Martha Deborah Hall
So Long

Winter's
breeze fills the air.
I'm so often alone.
The crowd inside me chants, "I can
do this."

Aged Cardboard Masks

The narrowed, harrowed, tarred masquerade ones
of my childhood when I pretended not to hear
parents screech nor care. The ho-ho, ha-ha,
"sexy" party disguise worn at the Phi Gamma Delta
frat party when the pre-med big shot laid me
in his dorm room. The party one worn each year
in Amherst Village as I pass out Milky Ways
to over a hundred Halloweeners. The lilting feather one
I wear in front of friends' husbands I don't respect.
The "I'm stupid, please fill my gas tank" one
I wear at Ralph's Exxon Station. The "blue Mondays"
paintball one that never hides the truth,
as I hang laundry on that day. The goalie mask
I wear to defend myself in my game.

Final Inning

It's not time to extrapolate.
Play your game. Run toward your goalpost.
It's not time not to extrapolate.
Race your game. Don't pontificate.
Who said you must always placate?
Forge toward your dreams. Score your utmost.
Race it. Do not extrapolate.
Play your game. Win at life's goalpost.

Part Three:
Before the Last Shoe Drops

Apart at the Seams

It hasn't been a tailored interface,
my move toward age seventy.
But I mended frayed cuffs, stitched
unraveled hems, buttoned myself up
to protect. This mender had been able
to double back folded parts along the way.
Some gatherings broke loose but on the whole,
designs held like Velcro and zippers
on winter jackets. Then stitches came undone.
A needle pricked my fabric, pleats ripped away,
my inner lining growing thin, my Singer
depleted of golden thread.

Martha Deborah Hall
Taps?

It slams through mahogany front doors,
sits in the living room, scatters
into different corners, then slithers
into life's full-length mirrors.

It will not be denied, insists on winning.
How will you deal with the mouse droppings
of old age? Will you leave them, cover them,
ignore them, or do away with the perpetrators?

Will you look out from rooftops or migrate
to damp basements. Will you dwell on delicious
autumns, wed your soul and spirit, or linger
in the tomb of an icy day? Will you rise

each morning, dive from bed to life,
or loll forever, ruminating over what
could have been? Do you face each day
with a "common sense breakfast from a time

when common sense was common"*
or throw in the towel every day around 9 a.m.?
Do you choose black or white, or what falls
in between? Do you stay or go, say yes or no,

act or punt, sing or cry? Do you do or don't,
ask why or why not, wed or divorce, stop
on the pavement or proceed? Will you give
or take? It is up to you.

*Kellogg's Corn Flakes ad.

Before I Lay Me Down to Sleep

What presents
will I bring to the end
of all my seasons?

What will they carve
on the stone block
waiting for my name?

I have been good
at taking. Better
start to learn the giving.

Martha Deborah Hall
Christmas Gifts in Year-Round Wraps

Welcome to the OFC (Old Friends Club).
We currently have four members, including me.
At seventy, I'm the youngest member of this clan.
I'm told Marnia, our newest member, is eighty-five.
I can't wait to meet her. We all live
in the same condominium complex and all drive
ourselves (and I'm not just talking about cars).

Membership requirements include a willingness
to trot, prance, and drudge through each other's
turmoil. Each must relay his or her ten-block story
to allow past sad occasions and transgressions in life
to go by-the-by. We must act in the now,
always show spine, realize there's no free rent.
Unhappy yesterdays aren't allowed to simmer.

Other membership requirements are simple, succinct.
We must be each other's Christmas bulbs, race horses,
flower parades, and shiners of rusted dreams.
We're watcher-outers against all bad luck, guiding prayers
for one another. We'll share ski poles and walking canes
when needed, serve éclairs on good-old-day plates,
as if we're kids just home from school. We must be

each other's confetti on days when there's no breeze,
daffodils that keep blooming when it rains. We must leap,
like reindeer, when we see one another, be the banding aid
of each other's torn hearts. We're not allowed to go south
in winters to loll on Florida beaches. As New Hampshire
Nordics, we'll stay north, break open a bale of hay, enjoy
the baying of a friend's goat. Over time we must hold on

Heading Toward Silver Dust

to the courage to live, be buttons on each other's jackets,
make each other's zippers slide easily up and down,
friends through all seasons. In spring we'll share
root beer floats, in summer, fresh lemonade, in autumn
hot chocolate topped with you know what. In winter
steaming chicken bouillon will warm the wintry mix.
We'll share freely our good, our bad, plough together

through ruts in the road, help each other to survive
incurred sadness. Gladiator, do you care to join?
If yes, we'll meet you on the veranda.

Martha Deborah Hall
Remember Me?

Two friends this week,
one did, the other didn't, ask me
to pray for them. After four years of respite
one refused to start chemo again. The other one
has sharp pins and needles streaming down
her left arm from shoulder blade to finger tips
and into her spine. "Pray for relief," she requested.

I don't mean to chant the B note of betrayal
to either friend, but I stopped praying
at an early age. Remember when I swirled off
the piano stool and got a babysitting job
at nine years old, blaring from life's orchestra pit
to the top balcony, "I can do it." I rarely ask another
to assist me, won't chant to a welfare office for help
with my self-composed opera in life. I try to look in
the mirror and see a face of self-expressed accord
and resonation. Life is an art you can compose
on your own. So I keep trying to create
and compose Acts I-IV of my opera, try to sing
the clearest, highest notes I can. I attempt to unwind
dissonant D-flats, reel my voice to the world
even though life may ultimately not applaud
my achievements. I'm my own Waldorf Auditorium.

So I closed the Venetian blinds on prayer, am my own
pounding hammer, try not to invite deadbeats
into my audience. I'm my self-written prayer,
throw others' fickle notes into violin cases,
try to leave any concert hall filled with notes
of dissonance. But Dear God, please help them both.
That's not a prayer. It's an order.

Let Your Hands Be

Bumble bees that buzz when you talk,
Appliers of a lipstick that covers ugliness,
United in prayer while thanking God,
Huggers of friends,
Holders of the microphone when you stand to sing.

Martha Deborah Hall
In Order

In autumn, let me be
a butterfly that lights and stays,

a wasp that has stopped
its stinging, a mosquito

that will not leave an itch,
a fly that knows when

it annoys, a moth that doesn't
darn holes. Let me form

a constellation to shelter
the whirling of my being.

My Retirement Vacation

April snakes out.
Bees sting.
Crows continually caw.
Forecast warns of constant rain.
King crabs knock about.
Maybe I shouldn't have left that job.

Martha Deborah Hall
Red-Roofed Retirement Cave

Blueberries for supper in plastic cups.
Kangaroo-like pockets hang on walkers.
Scrambled-egg smears show on worn books.
A synthetic bedspread's slung over a door.
Strewn on a shelf: Hershey Bar wrappers.
The day I arrived, I ran out of gas.
The once solid me rots inside.
Beyond my patio's concrete wall,
a spring garden wants back in.

Before the Last Shoe Drops

Allow me to
bask in strawberry
Crocs,
find apricot-colored
hay in my pocket,
know not to pretend
it wasn't the real
me.

Martha Deborah Hall
Clone This

A winter soon bumps into spring.
Blue dusk waits around the corner.
Corner your anger. Stomp it out.
Don't forget to "girl talk" with your friends.
Elvis tapes can still be *Brooklyn-Bopped* to.
Fudge is good for you on rainy days.
Give some of those old high heels to charity.
Hydrangeas bear sterile white flowers. Like you?
It's fragile, this thing we call life. Treat it with respect.
Jackknives should still be kept in your pockets.
Keep a hammer in that old toolbox of yours.
Let the crowd inside you prance outdoors.
Monday mornings don't have to be blue.
New fashions aren't always up to date.
Old timers aren't necessarily antiques.
Practice for heaven if you believe or if you don't.
Question authority. It's about time.
Remember the salty taste of the ocean, trout swimming in the pond.
Spring seasons, if good, should be frozen in hearts.
Take a winter morning walk as often as you can.
Undertake the hardest task first.
Validate yourself for once. You're worth it.
What's what is what.
Xylose? I'm eighty and have never seen this word before.
You should still sing aloud "The Star-Spangled Banner."
Zoos can be fun for oldies, too.

Not Old Fogeys

The whirling of slamming treadmills overcome,
Still crossing the deepest rivers.
We're vivacious sunflowers never thwarted by tractors.
With salted attitudes, we forge ahead.

Martha Deborah Hall
January Mantra

Of the twelve months,
January describes me best.
It's January twenty-sixth
of my eightieth year.
On one day, I can be cold,
on another warm. I can steer
streams of melting water
into drains or grow gutter icicles
that look like knives. Resolutions
made on New Year's Eve can be broken,
and usually are. I can go it alone
on slippery walkways or tote ski poles
for support. I can sport fleece mittens
on the fifth of the month or go without
like an ignorant toughie. I can daily
pick up strewn newspapers
or allow them to languish until April
Fools. I can rise up and glide through
new fallen snow or stay inside and turn
my back. I can neglect the world
in which I live or welcome it inside
to sit by the fire.

Like Cheetahs

Embers in a fire still give off good heat.
Release us from this tomb they call old age.
Let us embrace this last segment of life's page.
Don't store antique china in rumble seats.

Old timers are often very upbeat.
We're in a new developmental stage.
Don't sequester us as in a bird cage
even if we do sometimes drag our feet.

Don't treat us like silver hair is a pox.
Let inner lanterns guide us on our way,
light our essences each and every day.
Let us say what we mean, mean what we say.
Make barren forever that old, black box.
Please keep unfairness toward elders at bay.

Martha Deborah Hall
Coffin Pillow Talk

No roses on my coffin, please.
Send them to folks in old-age homes.
Let acts of hate forever cease.
No roses on my coffin, please.
Please leave my bones in graceful peace.
Let seeds of love sow in death's loam.
No roses on my coffin, please.
Bring them to folks in old-age homes.

Whose Engine Will My Leftover Car Keys Start?

Who will guide my leftover Volvo onward,
fill my gas tank when it starts to run on empty?

Who will follow past stops and starts
along my way, steer my auto's engine

once my trip nears its final destination?
Who will sort through all the good things

I've traveled for? Who will replenish
these tired tires, almost out of air,

accelerate and power-wash hopes
I took a stand on? Who will storm

the interstates with my dreams,
with the speedometer reading eighty

along the way? Will someone find
in the glove compartment my license

for life? Or will secretly-wrapped dreams
float into the air, or be rinsed clean

like dirty rubber mats at the car wash?
Will another release my clutch, recheck

my engine, forget to change the oil? Shall I
choose someone else to turn off my headlights?

Or shall I, at the end of my road trip, drag along
in life as a used spare?

Martha Deborah Hall
"Keys That Are Used Do Not Rust"

Albanian proverb

Celebrate life; create each day.
Uncover the you in your art.
Gracefully dance to your ballet.

Your performance is your sorbet.
All essences boldly impart.
Celebrate life, waltz in each day.

Creation parlays life's forays.
Create like you are a Mozart.
Dance with all heart in your ballet.

Write it down, point out life's forays.
If you stumble in scenes, restart.
Celebrate life, chant in today.

Perform with grace in your ballet.
Truth is a thing you can't outsmart.
Let your painting be your parfait.

Let your works fly on life's runway.
Create your tune with soul and heart.
Celebrate life, act like it's May.
Dance gracefully in your ballet.

About the Author

Martha Deborah Hall's poems appear in numerous national journals including, Bellowing Ark, Common Ground Review, Las Cruces, Old Red Kimono, Tale Spinners, Tapestries, The Poet's Touchstone and Watch the Eye. She is the winner of the 2005 John and Miriam Morris Chapbook contest for her collection Abandoned Gardens. She was a semi-finalist in the 2007 Concrete Wolf Chapbook contest and a semi-finalist in the 2010 Kathryn A. Morton Prize in Poetry presented by Sarabande Books and one of five finalists in the Vernice Quebodeaux 'Pathways" 2010 Poetry Prize. Plain View Press published three books, Two Grains in Time and My Side of the Street in 2009 and Inside Out, published and nominated for a Pushcart Award in 2011. In 2012 D-N Publishing published White Out, Hall's book on suicide and drugs.

Hall was honored by the New Hampshire Poet Laureate to be one of NH's featured poets. She is a member of the Manchester New Hampshire Poets Unbound group. Her Chapbook The Garbo Reels was published by Pudding House Publications. She is a member of the Academy of American Poets and The Poetry Society of New Hampshire and the Monadnock Writer's Group.

Hall is a past President of the Amherst Junior Women's Club, was the Amherst Chairman for Ronald Reagan's bid for the presidency and was Communications Director for Alexander Haig when he ran for President. Hall holds degrees from Ohio Wesleyan University (Class of 1963) and Columbia University (Class of 1967) and is presently a Realtor with Coldwell Banker in Amherst, NH. Hall's books may be purchased through, Border's, Barnes and Noble and the Toadstool Bookstores in NH.

Martha Deborah Hall
Country Mansion Condos, Unit 6
135 Amherst Street
Amherst, NH 03031
603-672-0106
debhall1@myfairpoint.net
http://marthadeborahhall.com/

www.ingramcontent.com/pod-product-compliance
Lightning Source LLC
Chambersburg PA
CBHW052112070526
44584CB00017B/2448